DOGMAN VS. GOATMAN

by Alberto Rayo

CAPSTONE PRESS
a capstone imprint

Published by Capstone Press, an imprint of Capstone
1710 Roe Crest Drive, North Mankato, Minnesota 56003
capstonepub.com

Copyright © 2026 by Capstone. All rights reserved. No part of this
publication may be reproduced in whole or in part, or stored in
a retrieval system, or transmitted in any form or by any means,
electronic, mechanical, photocopying, recording, or otherwise,
without written permission of the publisher.

Library of Congress Cataloging-in-Publication Data is available on
the Library of Congress website.

ISBN: 9798875225604 (hardcover)
ISBN: 9798875225550 (paperback)
ISBN: 9798875225567 (ebook PDF)

Summary: Two swift cryptids prepare for a fierce battle.
Who will come out on top, Dogman or Goatman?

Editorial Credits
Editor: Ashley Kuehl; Designer: Hilary Wacholz; Media Researcher:
Rebekah Hubstenberger; Production Specialist: Tori Abraham

Image Credits
Shutterstock: cammep, 29 (crown), Daniel Eskridge, cover,
9, 10–11, Eric Isselee, 19, GSoul, 17, HWWO Stock, 27, JM-MEDIA,
5 (bottom), 13, 14–15, 25, kostiukart, 26, MDV Edwards, 7, Michele
Korfhage, 20, Obsidian Fantasy Studio, 29 (dogman), Raggedstone,
21, Warpaint, 5 (top), 6, Werewolves 3D illustration, 23

Design Elements
Getty Images: iStock/AdrianHillman; Shutterstock: Ballerion

Any additional websites and resources referenced in this book are
not maintained, authorized, or sponsored by Capstone. All product
and company names are trademarks™ or registered® trademarks of
their respective holders.

Printed and bound in China. 006276

TABLE OF CONTENTS

FURIOUS FIGHT! 4

LOOK-ALIKES 8

CANINE CRYPTID 12

GETTING HIS GOAT 18

CLAWS AGAINST HOOVES 22

Glossary 30

Read More 31

Internet Sites 31

Index 32

About the Author 32

Words in **bold** are in the glossary.

FURIOUS FIGHT!

A strange noise breaks the forest's quiet. Is it a dog howl or a human scream? Two **swift** figures run through the dark woods, exchanging blows and scratches. When the moon shines down, they see each other clearly. One is a dog. The other one is a goat.

No, wait. One is Dogman. And the other is Goatman. These **cryptids** are ready to brawl!

Name: Dogman

Aliases: The Michigan Dogman, the Beast of Bray Road

Type of Cryptid: Dog-like humanoid

First Sighting: 1887

Range (Area): Michigan and Wisconsin

Likes: Howling, leaping huge distances, running fast

Dislikes: People, crowded areas, daylight

Name: Goatman

Aliases: Pope Lick Monster, Sheepman, Lake Worth Monster

Type of Cryptid: Goat-like humanoid

First Sighting: 1957

Range (Area): Kentucky, Texas, Maryland

Likes: Railroad bridges, eating dogs and farm animals, scaring people

Dislikes: Dogs, people in cars

LOOK-ALIKES

Dogman, as his name suggests, is a **hybrid**. He's mostly human but with a dog's head, snout, and sharp teeth. This creature is about 7 feet (2.1 meters) tall. His glowing eyes look yellow . . . or sometimes blue. Dark, thick fur covers his body. Big claws help him hunt.

Goatman is also a hybrid cryptid. He has a goat-like head, two big horns, and hooves. Sometimes he copies human voices. He's been known to harm dogs and attack cars. Sometimes he throws dogs at cars!

FACT
Pan is a character from Greek **mythology**. Like Goatman, Pan is part goat, part man. He's also a famous trickster!

CANINE CRYPTID

Both cryptids live in the United States. Dogman has mostly been seen in Michigan. But sometimes he goes to Wisconsin too. In that state, he visits Bray Road. So people there know him as the Beast of Bray Road.

Dogman attacks any human that gets too close to his forest habitat. Sometimes wild dogs help him.

SHIFTING SHAPES

Odawa people have lived in Michigan for thousands of years. Their stories are passed down through generations. These tales tell of shape-shifters, or humans that can change into animals. One Odawa tale describes a medicine man who turned into a dog. But he never changed back!

FACT
The Odawa, also known as the Ottawa, are an Indigenous people from the Great Lakes region of North America.

FACT OR FICTION?

In 1987, Michigan radio host Steve Cooke wrote a song about Dogman. He included details from stories of local people who had seen the cryptid. The song, called "The Legend," was meant to be a joke. Cooke didn't think the stories were true. But then people called him to say they had seen Dogman!

FACT

It's possible that some Dogman sightings were really bear sightings. A bear that has shed its fur would look like a tall, thin human.

GETTING HIS GOAT

Goatman has been seen in Kentucky, Texas, and Maryland. He doesn't wait for humans to get close before attacking. He even leaps on cars to scare the people inside. He's also been known to kill farm animals.

FACT
Some Goatman sightings may be cases of mistaken identity. People may have seen deer, bears, or other animals and thought they were the cryptid.

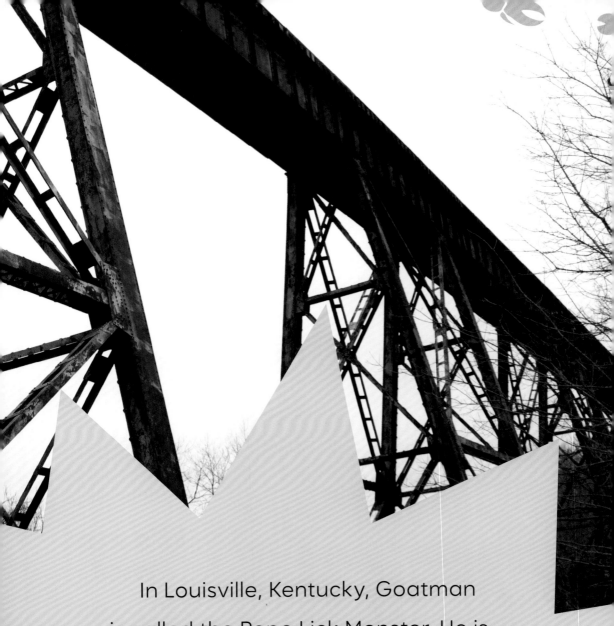

In Louisville, Kentucky, Goatman is called the Pope Lick Monster. He is said to **lure** people to the Pope Lick railroad bridge. People have accidents there, often deadly ones.

One story tells of an **abandoned** baby. He was a hybrid goat-human. The baby was adopted by a traveling circus. But that family abused him. The adult Goatman finally escaped during a huge train crash on the bridge.

CLAWS AGAINST HOOVES

Back to our furry fight. Dogman jumps toward Goatman, claws ready to slash. A swift kick from Goatman's hooves stops Dogman's leap. That kick was strong! Dogman fights back with his superior speed.

Goatman's strength could help him win. But Goatman isn't fast enough to hit his enemy a second time.

Goatman's hooves could knock Dogman down with a single kick. But first Dogman must let his guard down. A short pause in the fight gives them both time to breathe.

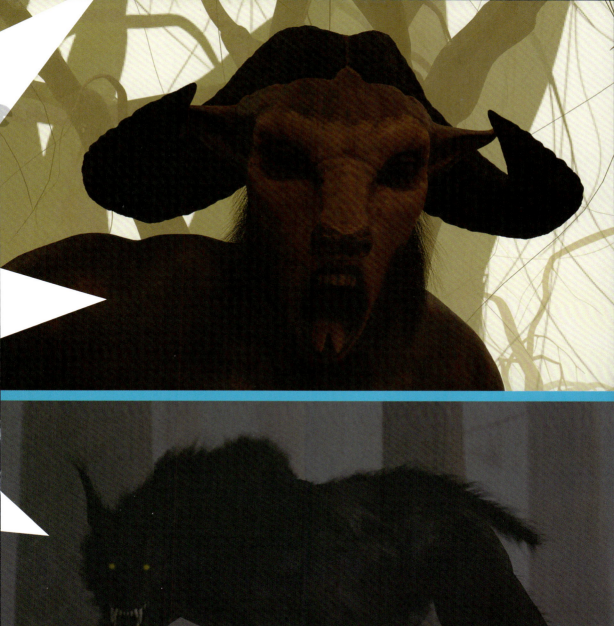

CLOSE COMBAT

Goatman attacking Dogman headfirst is risky. One false move and Dogman could **maim** Goatman.

Dogman's claws won't do enough damage to quickly defeat Goatman. But Dogman's powerful jaws might lead him to victory. Who will attack next?

Dogman lunges forward. His teeth sink into Goatman's shoulder. Goatman is stuck! He cannot use his horns. Dogman doesn't let go. He bites harder! Badly hurt, Goatman gives up.

IT'S OVER! DOGMAN WINS!

BUT DO YOU AGREE? Who do you think would win when

Dogman and Goatman CLASH?

GLOSSARY

abandoned (uh-BAN-duhnd)—having been left or given up on

cryptid (KRIP-tid)—a creature whose existence has not been proven

hybrid (HYE-brid)—a combination of two animals or species

lure (LOOR)—to tempt or attract

maim (MAYM)—to permanently harm a part of the body

mythology (mi-THAH-luh-jee)—a group of stories that belong to a particular culture

swift (SWIFT)—moving or able to move very quickly

READ MORE

Breach, Jen. *Mythical Monsters*. Greensboro, NC: Rourke, 2024.

Finn, Peter. *Do Monsters Exist?* New York: Gareth Stevens Publishing, 2023.

Yorke, Malcom. *Beastly Tales*. New York: DK Publishing, 2023.

INTERNET SITES

American Museum of Natural History: Mythic Creatures Challenge
amnh.org/explore/ology/anthropology/mythic-creatures-challenge

Atlas Obscura: International Cryptozoology Museum
atlasobscura.com/places/international-cryptozoology-museum

The Legend of the Michigan Dogman: A Modern Werewolf Tale
discoveryuk.com/mysteries/the-legend-of-the-michigan-dogman-a-modern-werewolf-tale/

INDEX

attacks, 10, 18

bridges, 7, 20, 21

cars, 10, 18
circuses, 21
Cooke, Steve, 16

Dogman
  behavior, 12
  features, 8, 27
  nicknames, 6, 12
  sightings, 6, 12, 16, 17
  stories of, 14, 16

farm animals, 7, 18

Goatman
  behavior, 18
  features, 10, 24
  nicknames, 7, 20
  sightings, 7, 18
  stories of, 21

Odawa people, 14

Pan, 10

shape-shifters, 14
songs, 16

ABOUT THE AUTHOR

Alberto Rayo is a writer from Lima, Perú. He loves science fiction that feels like fantasy, fantasy that feels like science fiction, and monsters (because they're cooler than humans). When he's not writing comics, he's writing prose. And when he's not writing prose, he might be sleeping.